The Madman
in this House

The Madman
in this House

Ishaq Imruh Bakari

Smokestack Books
1 Lake Terrace, Grewelthorpe,
Ripon HG4 3BU
e-mail: info@smokestack-books.co.uk
www.smokestack-books.co.uk

ISBN 9781838465308

Smokestack Books
is represented by
Inpress Ltd

'…we carry
Each of us an urn of native
Earth, a double handful
anciently gathered.'
Christopher Okigbo

Contents

New Planet
of the Apes

Pleased to meet you, El Negro

El Negro
Died circa 1830
Carried away to Europe in death

No one dared to remove
the stuffing pasted
in the place of intestines
tamed to serve the saviour.
The title tag marks
a warrior caged
in glass box sealed
just enough to keep
decorations in view
a substitute for a tomb
awarded to an unknown
but many times, named
and willed to be always
present and labelled.
He must bear witness
as object being
standing still for years
never wetting the carpet.

Pleased to meet you
El Negro, after so long
weathered by world
travel and mascot care.
Names mispronounced
lost here and there
your fragile frame
listed with possessions
found by a hitch-hiker
lost in a small town of little
people and the windmill
voices of one-eyed effigies

scolding children with black
faced things that work well
for a good Christian burial,
just in case
a dance of African drums
might come to the rescue.

And finally, the boxed
delivery from showroom
heaven, fuzzy hair is all
that stood the test of time.
Repatriated fittings and fixtures
fortified in the consecrated
European mind a national
treasure was prepared to be
received into African soil
thankfully with colourful
umbrella against the sun.
The empty space left
behind may yet prove
useful for loose coins
and thoughts iced
in innocence
wedded to the dreamtime
reserved for noble causes.

El Negro
October 2000
Returned Home to African Soil

Apeicity

after centuries of giving
birth to monsters
(white) man decided
to take a bubble bath

an itching urge
to self-redeem seeps
from beneath the skin
needing to repossess
nirvana the inflated rubber dolly
designed to stimulate oneness

in the spent afternoon acid
tipped breakfast cereal
fills Christmas stockings
with nowhere to ease
the serenade of bloated bowels
floating in the mongrel whistle

the afterbirth makes
mummy motions
life transfixed in death
stutters across
minefields manured
in glitz seeking
respite in a plausible
plughole to asylum

the wheel!
eureka!
the wheel!

after centuries of soaking
in bubble (smeared)
mascara peels from el dorado
reflections hung out to dry

Mastermind

with a face
that frightens itself
his whiteness
stands out with
an electric hue

someone said he was
a genius born with turbines
fixed into sockets of settled
forget... fullness

there is nothing more deadly
than a promised pleasure plan
for a blind widow left holding
an expectant smile
anticipating a command
when something stirs
where captive Africans
stood in sinking sand

save the last
dance for me he sings
into the mirror
his hooked fingers
rolling gelded dice

his highness is perched
between the poise of rust
on auction block
and the posture of market
breeze raising
klu klux... klan dust

A Waltz of Penguins

...there is no other way to begin
without knowing the ending
but to embrace the daylight
like the light bulb as a friend
seated on a rock-line shore
where rivers meet the sea
and penguins take chances
waltzing in the surf

...there is no other way to swing
new habits into colonial
straightjackets hanging
out at home fence building
against the bleary northward
surge curdling a mass of old
traditions home-cured in trash
cans clattering in the chest

...you will make your bets on
passing odds and sods
the barrel ship of state loose
cannons and flailing tollgate
recommissioned in mothball
glamour you will wait
with the aftertaste uncovered
for the emperor's party

Siege of the Old Pirates

The doors are locked
bolted firm tonight
securing all plundered
possessions placed here for our comfort.
We will sit here cobwebbed in this autumn
country hoping there will be tunics, tightly
fitted to dazzle the reaper and the fear.

The guillotine is alert
at Britannia's windows
keen sentries stationed
in anticipation wait for the rumble outside.
The echo will eat its way up crimson carpet
to the imagined where septic claws lodge,
stripped between crevices of conversation.

Nightriders

The tee-shirt carries
a danger signal
worn inside out
there is no harm
it sells an airbrushed
soul to the condemned

Evangelical salesmen
arrive to cuddle
orphans reciting history
in running belly chants
sterilised to numb their organs
traded for tar baby promises

Friendly Zulus

Zulu, Zulu Dawn, and future reality remakes...

I
there is no mistake
the arrival is expected
a group of warriors lost
and toothless in the A-Z
will raise no alarm like lions
missing from a zoo would do

II
only the trace of a spear
in the picture is left
blunted by the last post
bugled off to mark
what remains of another
frazzled recreation day
the gathered flies inhabit
memory stalking
dinner briefly
interrupted they loiter

III
asked to perform
at friendly kindergarten
parties Exhibit A is brought
into service every now
and then it takes a curtain
call in examination halls
where butchers banquet
on the guts left behind

IV
hand in hand
snug inside her majesty's
regulation boots in service
the memorials retrace
the menu cards soaked
in the vintage taste of glory

for entertainment
warriors cloistered
in a green grass cock-tail room
can have all vexation vented safely
truth splashes around economically
in a purpose-built chatterbox pool

The Grenfell Tower Murderer

Somewhere behind
a door safe and sure
Somewhere behind
a fridge clad in comfort

At number sixteen
on the fourth floor
the murderer laid a plan
hand in hand a chain of beneficiaries
upright and without risk
managed the standards designed
to tinsel strut the strong and stable
appearances that matter

When scorched voices
sounded the alarm
a common language fought
the raging flames and smoke signs
the clear orders in English
that answered the unopened council
chambers the overflowing closet files
inked for social cleansing

> *symbolism is everything in politics*
> *nothing signifies like the significant*

The murderer took the heat
outside to taunt and tease
as smoke offered a blanket
to dry eyes and mouths paralysed
between floors wishing to speak
to be heard to live a little more
than foreign fingerprints trapped
by the betrayal of a gaping door

the royal borough has gone red
tears and time will count the dead

The murderer is prepared
there is snake oil in the scheme
of things masked in leopard skin
clothed wolves tagged to privilege
serve up parables in procession
as ventilation for deprivation
and austerity raising public school
buffoons a cut above the rest

new architects linger in the backdraught
voices keeping the stilled alight
in alabaster black an epitaph

to those who could not find refuge
in half-baked media cladding
speak clearly or speak back

A waterless fall
        of corpses finds meaning
In the searching anger rescued
        from trampled footsteps

The murderer mingles
in the miscounting of the deeds

Official and unofficial
suspects left casual and ballpark

The murderer mingles
in between the margins of profit

Somewhere
        behind an unapologetic anti-migrant march
Somewhere
        behind flowers clutched in sacred memory

The Scientist will be an Undertaker
on another Planet

your arrival is expected
the coming
the trinity
la Nina–Pinta-Santa Maria
swipe card hotwired
to the sacred
vaults of London
all is prepared for your liberation

from the earthly condition
the logic of maps made
in conquests the pyrrhic
march of western standard
time the invention of man
the value of your facts
fused into galaxies
of your own black hole

the rabbit-run is dressed
for rehearsal
retro tripping hippy
flowers in your hair
and the eggs your progeny
will lay in cellophane
the caskets of your last
ovation deserve
Nobel merit with alpine
chicken in celebration

bring your incantations
the address book of Galileo
his heretic sandals soaked
in Red Indian wine or rum
seasoned in an arctic sun
small fishes battered
bread the usual wrapped
lunch with allergies
for adults – pills and play
things they must want!

your arrival is awaited
the cloudburst
the thunder after
the prediction of transit
the selfie received
two solstices double
equinoxes your multiple
orgasms kitchen knives d-i-y

tools radiant and rising
waxing upward in motion
the team is in tact
Jean-Dinah-Rosita-Clementina
virgins trained to feed
cats late for dental
care and mentor
robots all well-balanced

in the scales of fair trading
and Hollywood apes
a new planet for Pilgrims
awaits with everything
that is thought to come
from out of space
the Mediterranean trafficking
the washed up debris
the discarded of the global
bartering and bloodletting

the pyramid selling
the deep mining
varicose paralysis caked
in crude sand all is not well
in your world without
end the amen splutters
vaporized in the waiting
for the reincarnation
for departure – promised
to the eternal destination!

The Dress Rehearsing Room

soon there will be
another long soprano
silent minute to contain
the tearing in the bone
a moment left
by an unwelcomed visitor
with bitter fruit
the writing on the wall
will sign itself into
the backdrop of enlightenment
manicured immaculately
dressed for another anniversary
lit with self-assured longevity

war brings people   together in purpose
with a promise that fuels   redemption in natural
selection war spreads   its essence a monster
bolted in the collar   bone its pagan faith
sanctifies trenches   with national pride
and ceremony   solid in self-certainty

for the apparatus roosting
in this rehearsing room
anthems are keenly drilled
with sterling silver
platter close
to hand holding memory
for reflection
no need to sing for supper
it comes ready
as destiny inflated to perfection
hunter-gatherers we all were
somewhere along the road
to this industrial efficiency

blood washed hands lounge
resting place
reflection kaleidoscopes
the currency of body count
where well placed cutlery
behinds rehearsing fake news

where booted feet find a
laced up in villainy
with rational formality
is calculated to be offered
rubs shoulders with fat
on the evolution of the mind

soon the long soprano
will find another gutter
in a voice among the scarecrow
anniversaries rolling into one
down the backdrop
to a fathomless womb
machined to precision
another bolt twisted to a whistle
making tracks along its journey
step by step counting
every carcass a trophy
dragging its costume
into eternity

Twilight Days

on the balcony of the twenty-first century
there is a man with a gun in his hand

wooden legs set
to one side in prayer
his prosthetics proliferate
with the agitation within

the man is sitting
shoes shackled to
another side torch lit in
ex machina intelligence

trigger happy he looks
at sweat drying sees nothing
but blood caking into the deep
trail travelled on rope tight for lynching

this is the BEAST
there in TWILIGHT days
the UNSETTLED decorum
takes on what is left of MAGNA
CARTA democracy and its MIMICRY
the TERMITES are RESTLESS
they bend BURNING crosses
into SWASTIKAS marching music
VOMITS all over the after-dinner BONES
KNIVES chime in PORK barrel speech

there is a gun in the hand
of a man his back to the bush
wooden legs grow in fields
trees stoop on stumps

The Flower in the Window

a silence stalks the headlines today
under a rain cloud of her wedding
dress the blind-date widow sits

she waits

she whispers through
a cracked looking glass
striving to decipher the brutal curve
persisting beyond the moon cycle

she prays for a flat line

neighbours intrude with their own
celebrations of gated celebrity
hoarded for posterity on CCTV

soul zest is lived
inside a body bubble

in this beginning
there is a tagged whistle-blower
caged like cactus in the mind
floating on ingested debris
he is the vain ledge
on an iceberg in remission
somewhere at a noon-time edge

in this beginning
there is a shroud forgotten
it measures the spaces keeping
footsteps apart searching
for a promise beyond
the widescreen tongues
tailored in their oily ease

...and the flower in the window
takes all light!

you have read the books and studied
well the must-have magic guide to ride
a cock-horse with fumble and fuddle
you have cultivated well the goose
steps trained in smart-work drills
flickering horizons into border grilles

now from memory's hatching rooms
a strange wind-draft strolls the high
street corridors where traffic lights
change guard with wired uncertainty
and sign-language narrations code
cut-price battles of beach life fantasy

the HD mirror on the wall
makes a tombstone slide
it fakes a fall
plays tricks with the clock
while the calendar counts
the blind date backwards

...and the flower
in the window
takes all light
needs no shade
it is shade!

Negotiating Positions in a Ten-Point Neo-Liberal Democracy Diagram

...as the madman
in this house

It has been decided
by committee to tie
you to a tree
and leave you free
to roam around

...for the storage room
sign the paying paper

It is just enough
to cover the bed
space over your head
and between to see
outside the window

...the committee can offer
a bargain for looking further

Count your blessings
calculate the profit
make a cheque out to
the loyalty points added on
the tax taken in advance

...the committee can suggest
a remedy for staying in touch

It is easier than thinking
which box is for ticking
in accepting the bargain winter
jabs or summer inspection
under sun bright surgical light

...the committee knows
you have no TV license

This amounts to a breach
of security something
deadly to prevent what
ever you may think is needed
to see outside the ticking box

...the committee regrets
the noises in the attic house

There is a debate running
wild Jack and Jill paddling
to stay up pulling bootstraps
tight with concern for security
and the word-slip above your head

...there are gifts wrapped
and hanging low

The soft slippers
above your head stuck
to the ceiling can be filled
with imagination to break boredom
or buy a paradise package holiday

...the details prescribed
have been removed

The fine print found
near your obituary flowers
for safety sectioned in watery
drip conveys a doctor's epigram
sip as slowly as necessary

...the occupants in the attic
house send down their love

It will all come together
on the thread that is your
tether to spice the rebellion
harbouring like flies on
the footplate that feeds you

...the vote which you have
given is kept in a safe place

In the event of war
your voice will be heard
spit in the drinking
bucket provided each time
a promise spends a penny

What to do...

What to do with the baobab
warrior pacing through
mismatched lyric syllables
the randomness is suspicious
feinting a foreign tongue tap
dancing beyond the barrenness
boldly offered...

It cannot be that nothing
just nothing is asked
no reward or charity
in heated anxiety no favour
or loaded gun searching
corpses of conscience
surrendered...

What to do with the itinerant
standing everywhere white
supremacy finds no pillar
or phantom virgin to hold
the sentry's 'Halt' or the flaking
fallacy of the blind sucking on
bloated infamy...

What to do... what to do...

The Impossibility of Being Black

*'BETWEEN me and the other world there is ever an unasked question
How does it feel to be a problem?'*

WEB DuBois, *The Souls of Black Folk* (1903)

On the twenty-fifth day of May
in the pandemic year of 20-20 clarity,
the attention span index was set
at eight minutes and forty-six.

> the alchemist rising
> to the occasion in the spotlight brings
> a raised hand
> claiming victory from the asphalt turf

On this day, the whatsup instapoly
graph speaks of another hero born,
in one short breath for *Man*,
a giant leap for misplaced faith.

> thank you, George Floyd
> unrestful-deadness flows abundantly
> from the silence seeping
> in the wailing solitude of a sorrow song

The gladiator, licks the wounds of his trophy,
sustenance held securely in the last
flutter of a chokehold, the prey speaks
with delicacy and sometimes difficulty:

*'BETWEEN me and the other world
there is ever an un*(answered) *question
How does it feel to be a* (dread-dub) *problem?'*

Desert
Storm

Droppings

The gifts   you have left
in your hasty   retreat
lay like shrapnel lounging
in the sparkle of persistent
pain and the mournful smoke
trailing to the water's edge

Now your smile
roosting in the full
moon makes a home
with no room
for air or echo

For the sentinel
there is licence
to recycle and reshape
the crocodile of a new
fashion statement

With handy halter   it will hold
everything to ransom

With bitter breath   it will measure
the probity of thirst

The gifts   you have left
in your hasty   retreat
the misplaced incendiary
the rose petals trampled
will be gathered in abundance
across a corrosive sea of ruins

The Monster Has Risen... Again

The monster has risen... again

somersaulting forward
awkward and blundering
camouflaged in media hype

As spectators our eyes
glow glazed by the shredded
paper trail of resolutions and conventions

The monster has risen... again

a cavalcade of death
in its wake across blackout cities
stripped of their sovereignty

As spectators we guard
our toes and fingertips jealously
bunkered in a ghostly night light

The monster has risen... again

in its wake
the fragile shadow boxing
the exile
the running away
the dislocated voices
in their loneliness

The marching band takes its toll
eating away at our silences

The marching band takes its toll
armour-clad and delirious

The marching band takes its toll
rattling into history

At the city limits
At the gate posts
At the sacred threshold
At the bleeding navel

By the rivers of Babylon
many lay down
their weeping wounds
So, step lightly
pirouette through
the minefields blossoming

Watch the new planet
grow up again debiting
the accounts of the natives

Watch the new planet
grow up again force
ripened and putrefied

The monster has risen... again

The trinkets... the threadbare veil

The conquistadors... the sea of stench...

The occupation... the... harvest...

The monster...

Force-Feeding in Guantánamo

This piece of tube
a wire in the age of wireless
is enough
is evidence
is testament
is oath of allegiance
is a kiss from the lips of the flag

It lends a hand in search
of a heart
or a hidden substance
somewhere certifying
the ration portion
the point of no return

This piece of tube
a wire in five-star general terms
is not a magic rope trick
is not mob justice
is not a contract signature
is not what you think
is not the screams you hear

It offers a resettlement
plan not too grand
but thoughtfully just
steered for motivation
it will twist and turn
in shape and motion

This piece of tube
wire in a forensic hand
takes account
finds the enemy within
settles scores
takes as long
as a piece of string

It provides a link
between piety
and the polity
it is a statement of fact
knotted to cement the footwear
of Western writ on track

This is a piece of wire
in the maelstrom of survival
it is clinically programmed
it is culturally treasured
it is all that is left
it is witness
it is whiteness

As long as a piece of string
this piece of wire
will make padded walls sing
in celebration with words
deep and guttural
across torturous scales

signs may wonder
as thoughts may
in time come
to rest the case

War in a Time of Terror

As I read the signs
here ordinary
in the everyday
war is heard marching
high on johncrow appetite
between the demons and disciples
in tow the cloaked patriotic parodies
tyrannies and passion plays parade
in bloodstained litanies

alarm bells clamour with the rock
and rolling bric-a-brac
the wheel-barrowed flourish
bringing home false flags
and Trojan horses

metal honoured desert rogues
carry their own red carpets
wrapped for any adoring bride
sleep walking in the pride
of foreign affairs

high on alert
spin doctors
work overtime
stoking the perennial
pantomime pushing
pass in the murmur
of ticking bullet boxes

containment and contentment
go hand on heart seeking
solace in stiff drinks draining
sediments of gallantry
with pomp and pageantry

When terror comes
roaming between sidewalks
it takes a cold stare
with eyes dispossessed
and reflection deferred
between the headlines and graffiti
the concealed fears and fantasy
beware the comfort offered
by ranting lords and majesties

Bread in a Time of Terror

if I asked you
for bread
would you say
that it needs
salt to taste
would you say
have it with honey
butter or spread
something more deserving
would you say
better still wait
until it is comfortable
and the right time
for bread
would you ask
what kind of bread
wrapping would I like
would you
say I am ignorant
and should know
that what I really want
must have a name
X-Y-Z in colours
of the ingredients
embedded into the date
of its afterlife
after which
it will become cake
or cork
with a barcode that says
bread does not belong
to all in the free
world of choice

would you ask
for my sake
for my protection
against
pity and embarrassment
what am I intending to do
with this bread

Homecoming for Mehdi

homecoming takes many forms
sometimes
a stranger arrives
with a familiar
smile yet nothing fits
the things left behind
a new smell marks
the blossoms
long abandoned on the road
to *pied-noir* valediction

sometimes shivering ghosts
appear
with laughter bloodied
by an unrecorded rape
bearing scars
old with anger
dispossession comes
gift-wrapped in a delirious
liquor loosened dance
all that is left after the odyssey

in a tsunami surge the prodigal
returns
as prophesy breaking
sound barriers built
to block
the cortege
moaning in the republic dust
the parade is here
bearing the begotten seasoned
and cold stored in amnesia

homecoming takes many turns
gathering
menace to its appointed place
it will take a transit
through the *banlieues*
sidestepping the gendarmes
between curfew
foyers like clockwork
it will sprocket tally
every colonial atrocity

Wailing Palestine

They sing today
plaintive melodies of death
in Gaza stripped to the bone
with flesh stinking and ragged

They sing today
discordant choruses of war
without end

There are no answers
for the children who ask
to know their names
There is no echo
for the laughter that should
embrace in showers

The rights of victims ride
On the eagle wing of predators

The rights of tyrants arrive
Cloaked in the gun-ships of crusaders

They sing today
discordant choruses of war
without end

Complicity is the pay per view
price for the pleasure
as the curse of 1948
dances everywhere
And the sycophants
parade to the chilling
tune of Palestine's pain

Wailing Palestine Vinyl

There are moments
        when sunlight protrudes
Through the scorched
        bones of martyrs
Now the entertainment season is here
        again with narcissistic zeal
And scrambled lullabies
        climb the hit parade

Gaza and Rain

Gaza, the world as you find it
is what the world wants
to talk about

good news on a bad day
the scales of injustice
are tipped to perform
balanced broadcasting at its best

no apologies
for the limping liberal
voices assured in certainty

no apologies
for the rampaging rodents
gowned and groomed in impunity

behind iron shield
and the guilt of complicity
the machine is primed
to explain the fever of the plague

Gaza, the world as you find it
is occupied land
to be procured

with funerary flare
well-groomed puppeteers
raise emboldened bulwarks
to sprout around the gated colonies

Gaza, the world as I find it
in cries and sacrificial
embers whispering

chimes another season
soaked in splintered slogans

stunted by the terror that lurks
where the acid of occupation rains

From the Ashes of a Map

for Fida Qishta

In some fairy tales
your homeland
is a land of broken
cameras countless
as the eyes of children
wrapped in dusty shrouds

In some fairy tales
your homeland
is a never-never land
where phosphorous flames
have fire-cracked barren
pathways across flowered fields

Yet you speak of the mysteries
in a martyr's epitaph

here you say
there are loaded stories
where birds gather stones
smooth enough for flat bread
to rise and inhabit a home
that can be trusted not to burn

here you say
there are olive trees
to shade the seeker who takes
your hand across the creeping
barricades and the wreaths
requisition for the blackmailer's feast

There is a place you say
where the sun shines after sunset

And clouds are not the exiled
memory from the ashes of a map

here you say
the sky is not mangled
in the mist it covers all
with chequered shawl
Hirbawi woven
and unconquered

Refugee Stride

I
To be found out or
to be discovered
                    will either way
                    terrify the secret
                    lover midnight robber
A persisting stain
is the tell-tale
                    wake across
                    the waves white
                    washing daylight ruins

in the evidence afloat
some blade...
some blade, the pallbearer said

The twisted tongue
left in the lost and found
takes a cat walk all over
the never ending

There is a judicious
air about the body
odour as fermenting
dry goods break cover

in saturated rigor mortis
she speaks...
she speaks, from the grave

II
It should be
a rocking chair

facing cool breeze
not this whirlwind
pool of fool's gold
and the bottomless
view reflecting flat
from a mirrored moment
meant to soothe the skin

It should be
a mirror that smiles

smiles back with
clickety clack dancing
beside a passing train
not this down pouring
inside a shelter for shoes
that bind the wearer
to destiny inside a wall

Not this sea
and the carcasses

carcasses of hope
brought ashore
to shiver without
shade in cold sight
a picture waiting
to be unhinged or once
again Siamese-twined

Not this delay
at arrival again

and again in silence
but calm breaking
defiant and collected
unbroken and determined
to be called more
than somebody
numbered and numb

III
nameless I will come
and go waved by
the rising or setting sun
to make it worst I
will stare without
thinking without
sinking into this place
removed and contained
low batteries
hold a refrain snared
in tremors of an emergency
I will dial
a #tag handle
for a stray
horse with wings

IV
Soldiers, they are all
Soldiers...
and you, the shoulder
for the grinding stone
a cure for straight backs

Soldiers, what else
Could they be...
in this jungle world
hand-me-downs are tossed
from pirate's wreck

Soldiers, you said
A friendly voice...
no less here to serve
the greater balance sheet
framed in breeze block chic

Soldiers, the uniforms
Stand stiff...
against the brave
who will read the stars
deep in steamy sand

V

Prayer time
       by the wayside
Mementoes inside
       fill all available space
From where I bow
       the circle is complete
Infants speak
       for parents long gone
To lay cobbled tracks
       on some undocumented street
Knowing hands
       raise a tongue untamed
From where I stand
       guardians look
At the land behind
       upside down and sore
Both sides in flames
       and not much more
Be it a bridge
       or glistening silk
Be it a bastard
       or a whore
Let fate tempt
       heart's rising roar

Warri (Oware) Moves

Thinking Sharpe, Taking Shape

thinking sharpe
before making the wise
move the wooden seat will tell
in its seesaw of flashing
spirits and seeds shaping choices
for a lifetime

thinking sharpe
before making a trace
the careless hand will betray
the flip-flop stories
will not endure the heat of fate
worse than death

in the scheme of big people
business in the hush
when strong breeze blows
and lamp light flickers
the trail of count and capture
makes clear the sowing
that will come back
to matter in the after

taking shape
one-one
one-one
each in reckoning
will give
and take

Secrets in Steady Time Beneath Smooth Rock

I

Hausa welé-o
Hausa welé...

what did the Civilised expect to see:
the welcome party
watching expectantly amazed
full of grace and blessed
with their bounty from the sea

what did the Civilised expect to see:
head counting rosaries
walking on two feet
in Sankey melodies
from the belly of a beast

the pirates gave
account for unsteady
feet now on new
ground all stock lost
between le(i)dge(su)r(e)
columns settled amicably

the sweet perfume of landed
goods filled the nostril furrows
with a smell of hell fermented
between the port of no return
and the pisspot of their tomorrows

the three in one redeemed
itself by naming its property
to make amends on earth
as it wished to be done
in the next eternity

Hausa welé-o
Hausa welé...

Hausa welé-o
Hausa welé...

II
'the whole world is Afrika'
Black Uhuru

water marked inside
hard covers unknown
names came afloat as sure
as scheduled rains
return to feed life
shackled in the fetid air

in the footsteps of recovery
there is absence in the spaces
left behind the doors
that do not close gaping
windows baring all
in anointed body bags

Kromanti Cudjoe!
call you pickney-o
call you pickney

the raiders will return again
and again they will leave
no burial ground unturned
planting their corrosive coins
on one side the branded hands
on the other a basket of crabs

Kromanti Cudjoe!
call you pickney-o
call you pickney

in the footsteps of recovery
there is presence
in occupation the thunder
rolling down the years
in every bush will know
its calling and the nimble
tongue in every rock
will speak the tale of cities
built on the bed of bodies
stretched across the sea

Bongo yetu iko pale
Bongo yetu ipo hapa vile vile

III

Capoeira welé-o
Capoeira welé...
Capoeira welé...

...everything is stripped
to string as on arrival
I will take my chance
with gravity in a moment
of stillness tightly drawn
back to the eternal
I will take the first
command and then
the search between
heaven and the stars

...everything is surrendered
to the abyss where
words collide in a sigh
before birth that signals
the nowhere else
to go but up in circles
taking fire from the deep
the call invites a chorus
flick-knifed I smile between
goodbye and Ibo returning

Capoeira welé-o
Capoeira welé...
Capoeira welé-o
Capoeira welé...

                    IV
there is always
another hill
to climb

over...
always
...up

from below sea
level stepping
over ghaut and washed
down rock to sofa
stone the next reach
is a ridge for ease
to mount
misery call it what
you will
fertile and flamed
there is always another
hill born after volcano

feeling for the smoothness of stone
hearing the quake of drumming
inside the proclamation of mission
a mentor's medicine takes
its march across
new maps

it may have begun one foreday
morning when white and black
became clear damp blades
marked ancient names
to faces laid
out in waiting

at every horizon
there is always
a recall

study it hard...
study it hard
and know

Like in the Rain Passing

in the closeness squeezed
into the memory of a shoe
big enough for two small feet
it was customary to cut through
the cemetery and pass in good
time the hospital on visiting day

it was just a quick way
to take across
moonlight stories
of Anancy dressed
for an emergency
or a crossroad calamity
until a jackass bull scattered Granny's will
bursting from the Guinea grass
stuffing her death
bed pitching feathers
all over the federation cricket flannel
and we all get wash-way again like in the rain passing

some went full off with strong
wind and jet stream
some gone like a ball lost
beyond door knock and bush lining
some into a green mango silence
ducking the short cut that leads to hell

hell...where none can tell
how to pass
the crucifix of bagasse
how to pass
the jackass bull dancing

What Thing of Value...

what thing of value   will remain?
as epitaph to the encounter
after the ornamental finger
prints sealed in dry-rot   confessions
without memory
destined
for boneyard hole

what thing of value   will be left?
at the end of progress
after the ba(i)ted apologies
stacked in happy-hour   bounty
and swear words
embroidered
on suicide notes

    celebrities will make a show
    flashguns and low cut flesh
    will wallow in wine
    wade in the water
    rock with the flow

    dancehall caterpillars will sing
    from sequined caskets flying
    elephants will twist
    neckties and crocodile
    tears into a circus ring

what thing of value   will be enough?
to hold the rushing clamour
after the fizzy manumission
adorned in fish-net stupor   bull-penned
by Empire accolades
strangling
the Cimarron

The Pretence of Horses

Horses wear
shoes with nails
driven holding firm
the reminder of where
they belong

And so
the beast dressed
in the breeding of its burden
must bite the bit
and froth with privilege...

I am not a donkey
Therefore... I am

...must run and strut
its bridled message
in the past tense
roaring like a lion
king in pappyshow

Bay Road Slow Drag

it takes   in slow drag
time walking away
from the cenotaph   in the heat
it takes   not much time
without tailcoat wind
walking on surf
strides steady
treading back
to reach the treasury
building beyond
the money counter's
bare foot welcome seat
carbon copied to cope
with the crammed
cruise ships of crusoes

it takes   a few minutes
in thinking time
to roll the years past   the market built
to outlast   dry blood
the daily grind
the overseer
at the corner
of one eye inside
the headstone draped
in flag of state
it takes clear flight
unfazed by the sea
between crop season
the creaking tin
roof and better days

after all the years walking past bata
shoes that leak motionless as bone
it bends to exchange storm shutters
for a dollar passport picnic plan
who knows when the white house
palace drip from the glory sky will end

gurgling seawater speaks
in unnamed faces seawater
speaks gurgling in faces
stamped on beer crate cages

it takes   a few minutes
walking without
questions taking time   at sharp corners
curtained to conceal   the currency
of the new deal
from estate monument
to memory internment
in the treasury's copper
cauldron loss
and profit added up
to the difference
collected in the ocean
span across faces
driven by road march
in slow drag delirium

burdened by the smoke of prayers
are gifts too drunk for the soul
of songs that will on a good day
dare to throw flames across
the lines where puppet strings
play officially dressed mouth organs

another lifetime to be
rescued from the big-drum voices
lost in misdirected voices to be
rescued from another lifetime

The Tourist is Always Right

'No charge for US tourists who assaulted Police Officers...'
(WINN FM News report, 3 January 2019)

It is a new year
after Christmas morning
with unwashed hangovers
things have wound down
washed ashore blown in

A policeman is facing
a tourist man and woman
exercising their privilege
tired of cowpat pleasures
straw that has worn thin

The policeman in character
will come to know
the watchman of his supplications
living sequestered
in his borrowed costume

called to attention
in hotel no-man's land
mad house alley brawn
flexes for a spear or a slingshot
something mean to complete
the neutered bulge of government
issue regulations

called to attention
his plain clothes
commissioned into service
wraps a permanent smile
and milks handshakes

'Yes sah.
I-am-a-police-man-sah!'

the new year brings western
freestyle to the decorated
two slaps and the last lap
mas'man is dusted
down unwinding
into quayside drudgery

...is long time
Quashey no sight
a nice time, somehow
di dance kiarn pay fi di light...

yes...   hurricane or flambeau
bright...   inner or moonglow

for places where absent
heroes linger in derelict foundations

for the forbidden tales
displaced in weed-infested corrugations

slicked back the sharp
edges of steel   drums are velvet coated

music is safety pinned
to jiggle bell   the island's honourable

nice...
is nice it nice!
Come again.

The Lions Lie

(Monty Python votes, and leaves for the Cari-beyond...)

where flag poles
wave like big sticks
peacocks and estate yard jump
up masquerades know their place

where unbuttoned
ends meet between
remitted tin roofs decorative
ebullience is dolloped duty free

> stone bound
> the *British*
> lions lie
> in a public square
> pigeons crown
> their greatness
> pythons dodge
> traffic
> > cross
> oceans
> > transit
> time ferreting
> for a return
> to fiefdom scent
> or a treasure cove
> of *Imperial* bones

in the master's voice
a *Pitchy Patchy* soliloquy
purposeful and polite
will proffer a welcomed
memory as if by ventriloquy
dressed in liturgies of faith
folded into harboured
smiles docked to greet

      all protocol
               observed
      the lions lie

The Elephant Never Forgets

The elephant never forgets
the weight of its own
memory moulded on a night
when one mosquito danced
with fire flies to make moon
light turn delirious double
vision into a prison room

The elephant never forgets
the circus master's favour
whip hand outstretched
water laced with sugar
and a key to secure safety
from the mosquitoes dancing
at a distance noisily

The elephant never forgets
lessons learnt by stress
and strain that stretched
the brain thin with shock
that sucked its trunk into timid
strength thinking with its tail
and the wrong end of the whip

The elephant never forgets
the grip of sitting soundly
on a rider reared on habit
who commands without question
nowhere near Hannibal
in wisdom just a duck for sitting
on when stripped of all illusion

In the Season of Topple and Tumble

Spreading, the stiff neck muzzle is put
to flight as locust creatures break cover.
The clamour unravels the amazing grace,
trailing hollow gods.

in the season of topple
and tumble perplexed treacle
tears hang in chains – trailing
into a winter palace life built
on rose garden graves – a smell
of contagion fumes like leather
soaked for whipping – sugar
stains the new imperial plan

Spreading, icons splash with dumbbell sound
missing the last dearly departed merchant ships.
Empire glory sinks into a scrap metal mist,
scoundrels dethroned exit.

To be...

for the Coltranes

...push the weight
against the edifice
bend its knees
into the ground
to buckle under things
will change must

change like persistent
shadows at midday
sliding around the bleak
room of promises
push the swinging
doors of peep

show mirrors framed
with a scavenger's coat

the knotted stethoscope
the blotted raffle tickets

push...

was all I heard
until a scream
stood
upright in the air
above to be...

Madikizela-Mandela

You have grown to know
The stadium
The mixing and the mingling
Mixed up in the rainbow and the toxic rain

You have grown to know
The colours
Dressed in combat camouflage
Where sechaba promises wait to be delivered

when the nation wakes
to rise and walk in your footsteps
the pillars bearing
the weight of tears
that surf you home
will bloom from the birdsongs
you have crafted with messages
wrapped and woven into an ageless
backbone tutoring timeless hands

You have grown
And you have shown the way
Is a bold distance beyond the bull
Bartering and the business as usual

You have grown
And you have taken the world
Strides further into a distance beyond
False dawns cradling headless chicken skins

You have grown
As a wellspring in the African ocean
As a winged voice in the river of Abantu
Eternal in the air and the life within its heart

Mamadou

...on the morning after massa
day was done
Mamadou sent a message
to simply say

Mi wan fi goh home...!

from his pocket
he took a tobacco
pouch hiding his name
a piece of cinnamon stick
for cleaning his tongue
and a soothing paadnah
hand of five-finger bush

as a free man
he could put the pig
foot out of the way
and say this is not for me
leave it near the cross
to be carried by whoever
cared to take it up

he had built
a house that stood
on stilts so he could
watch more clearly get
the changing wind sight
mongoose and slithering
snakes working overtime

he was a man
who could see
what others heard
and speak to heal all
things except death
or the mashup head inside
double cross emancipation

...on the morning of the day
after the free paper blew away
in the dust swept from plantation
to make room for compensation

Mamadou was found
in donkey rope bound
holding the last stilt left
in the ground of his house

burning grief
and threats carried
far and wide on the tobacco smell
mixed up in cinnamon and bush balm

...hiding his name until this day
some simply say

Huh... dat man was dangerous!

Among the Tea House Whispers...

for Sidi Fuad Nahdi

in a heart lived deep
among the tea house whispers
in the crowded loneliness
carpeted on a baraza of baraka

You walked slowly
and talked one pace ahead with fire fuelled eloquence
your measured strides burnt
new light across spurned pathways in desolate ground

Like food for thought
precious things were table spread like a tasbih puzzle board
find here room for all
the exalted names, the companions and the generations

and for those who by fate
fashion or design
would turn up late a sign
said take your time
the cinnamon stick said sharp
knives do not always draw blood

There is always
a fireside in winter chill or summer shade

In quiet reflection
choose as you will with the weight each fingertip can bear

taking nothing
but the gifts
threaded through
an effervescent life

there are jewelled
moments to be
retraced into the future
as the seeker journeys on

Centenary Jam

for Coleridge Goode at 100 years

Do not mistake
this occasion   for a duck and dive
Do not stumble
into this place   for cheap recreation

sponsored by those
who market mass ovation

In this formation
the intermingled
generations turn
to face the collected
gifts exchanged
across the seas
and waves of years

Do not mistake
this jam session   for a soft shoe shuffle
Do not stagger
into this celebration   for a frothy frolic

in a dingy cellar
waiting for a raid

This is no cakewalk
in the park or jig
up the hit parade
This is work to mark
a moment placing
into sequined spaces
patchwork pieces
designed to disrupt

bull dogs of the grand
illusion still swinging high
cross-legged and catacombed
in their entitlement

This is no singsong
for a sentimental sojourn

This is no sorrow serenade
to sanitize barbarity

Bad bass lines stomp
lightly taking time
to tell the tales
that will keep agile
warriors awake
in free formed landscapes
unfurled and on fire

Upright you stand
destiny in hand
stepping stones
have built new freedoms
with calypso sketches
simmering in the symmetry
of deep majestic tones

Do not mistake
this cool shade   for a palm tree
Do not stutter
in the silence waiting   for a 1-2-3 (4 time)

A rock without a frown
the raw strings of your bow
are spiced with colours
leading those that follow

Into the winged soul
guided by a diviner's gaze

Into the blue heart
woven with festive flair

Into the rhumba
root
Into the in-can-descent
glow

Notes

El Negro

El Negro or the Negro of Banyoles or El Betchuanas, a stuffed human from Botswana was displayed as a museum curiosity in France and Spain from 1830, and acquired by Spain's Darder Natural History Museum of Banyoles in 1916. In 1992, in the midst of preparations for the Barcelona Olympic Games, an international group of African individuals, including Alphonse Arcelin, 'Magic' Johnson, Kofi Annan and Jesse Jackson, with support from the Organisation for African Unity, called for its removal from the museum. In 2000 the human remains were eventually repatriated to Botswana.

Secrets in Steady Time Beneath Smooth Rock

'Bongo yetu iko pale/Bongo yetu ipo hapa vile vile' (Kiswahili) – Our (Africa) Bongo is there/Our (Africa) Bongo is also here. Some lines are adapted from the Carriacou Nation Songs, 'Hausa welé' (Hausa ambush) and 'Kromanti Cudjoe'.

Mamadou

This poem is inspired by an event recalled by Ray Chickrie and Shabnam Alli in 2016, in *Kaieteur News*, 'Mamadoe was burnt to death in British Guiana' and *Caribbean News Now!*, 'Mamadoe, the Muslim enslaved African burnt to death in Guyana'.

The images on page 5 are Adinkra symbols: Akoben/Abeng/War Horn (vigilance), Aya/Fern (endurance) and Dwennimmen/Ram's Horns (humility and strength).

Acknowledgements

Thanks are due to the editors of *Wasafiri*, where 'Wailing Palestine' was first published (2009).